Castles
of the World

# Biltmore House
## America's Largest Private Residence

### Ruth Daly

MEDIA ENHANCED BOOKS
AV2 BY WEIGL
ADDED VALUE • AUDIO VISUAL

www.av2books.com

AV² provides enriched content that supplements and complements this book. Weigl's AV² books strive to create inspired learning and engage young minds in a total learning experience.

## Your AV² Media Enhanced books come alive with...

Go to **www.av2books.com**, and enter this book's unique code.

## BOOK CODE

B 7 6 8 9 3 5

**AV² by Weigl** brings you media enhanced books that support active learning.

### Audio
Listen to sections of the book read aloud.

### Video
Watch informative video clips.

### Embedded Weblinks
Gain additional information for research.

### Try This!
Complete activities and hands-on experiments.

### Key Words
Study vocabulary, and complete a matching word activity.

### Quizzes
Test your knowledge.

### Slide Show
View images and captions, and prepare a presentation.

**... and much, much more!**

Published by AV² by Weigl
350 5th Avenue, 59th Floor
New York, NY 10118
Websites: www.av2books.com   www.weigl.com

Library of Congress Cataloging-in-Publication Data
Daly, Ruth, 1962-
 Biltmore house, : america's largest private residence / Ruth Daly.
    pages cm. -- (Castles of the World)
 Includes bibliographical references and index.
 ISBN 978-1-4896-3388-0 (hard cover : alk. paper) -- ISBN 978-1-4896-3389-7 (soft cover : alk. paper) -- ISBN 978-1-4896-3390-3 (single user ebook) -- ISBN 978-1-4896-3391-0 (multi-user ebook)
 1.  Biltmore Estate (Asheville, N.C.)--Juvenile literature. 2.  Asheville (N.C.)--Buildings, structures, etc.  I. Title.
 F264.A8D35 2015
 975.6'88--dc23
                        2015001369

Printed in the United States of America in Brainerd, Minnesota
1 2 3 4 5 6 7 8 9 0 19 18 17 16 15

032015
WEP070315

Editor: Heather Kissock
Design: Mandy Christiansen

Every reasonable effort has been made to trace ownership and to obtain permission to reprint copyright material. The publishers would be pleased to have any errors or omissions brought to their attention so that they may be corrected in subsequent printings. Weigl acknowledges Getty Images, Alamy, Corbis, Newscom, iStock, Wikipedia, and Dreamstime as its primary image suppliers for this title.

# Contents

# What Is Biltmore House?

Tucked away in the Blue Ridge Mountains of North Carolina is a grand mansion that rivals the castles of Europe. Biltmore House is the largest private home in the United States. It was built more than 100 years ago by George Washington Vanderbilt, whose family was one of the richest in America. Biltmore was built as a country house for Vanderbilt and his family. The house, along with the estate that surrounds it, were to be a place where the Vanderbilts could relax and spend time with friends.

Biltmore House is still owned by the Vanderbilt family, but it is no longer used as a home. The current owner is George Vanderbilt's great-grandson, William A. V. Cecil.

Biltmore House was also built to be a showcase for Vanderbilt's large art collection. As a wealthy man, Vanderbilt traveled to countries all over the world, collecting many paintings and antiques on his journeys. When Biltmore House was completed, he filled it with art and expensive furnishings. Today, people from around the world come to Biltmore House to tour the building and view the art on display.

Biltmore House receives more than **1 million** visitors annually.

The entire estate originally covered **125,000 acres** (50,586 hectares) of land.

Biltmore House has **250** rooms. These rooms include 34 bedrooms, 43 restrooms, and 3 kitchens.

**1,000 men** worked on the construction of Biltmore House.

# A Step Back in Time

Biltmore House was built during the Gilded Age of American history. This was a time of great economic growth in the United States. The wealthy became more wealthy, and many were generous with their money. These people built museums and other cultural institutions. They donated money to help others. They also built large houses for themselves. Vanderbilt grew up in grand homes, but he wanted his house and estate to be different. His goal was to create a community. Biltmore Estate was designed to include one large house, with farms and a small village close by. This community was to be self-sufficient and able to generate its own income through a variety of agriculture-based activities.

George Vanderbilt was 27 years old when construction started on Biltmore Estate.

**1888** George Vanderbilt visits Asheville, North Carolina. He decides it is the perfect place to build a country home. He begins to buy farms and other land in the area.

**1891** The first bricks and limestone for the house are put into place.

| 1880 | 1885 | 1890 | 1895 |

**1889** Vanderbilt buys the town of Best. He renames it Biltmore Village. Construction begins on the house and estate.

**1895** George Vanderbilt moves into his new home. Biltmore House officially opens on Christmas Eve.

Even though Biltmore House opened in 1895, it did not complete construction for several more years.

**1900** Construction of the Main Dairy and Horse Barn begins.

**1942–1944** The house closes during World War II and becomes a storage facility for artworks from the National Gallery of Art.

**1995** After several conservation projects, Biltmore House celebrates its 100th anniversary. Recently restored rooms are opened to the public.

**1900**      **1925**      **1950**      **1995**

**1914** George Vanderbilt dies. His widow, Edith, sells about 87,000 acres (35,200 ha) of the estate to the United States Forest Service. Today, this land is part of the Pisgah National Forest.

**1930** Biltmore House opens to the public during the **Great Depression**. It is hoped that tourists will visit the area and spend money.

**1963** Biltmore Estate is declared a National Historic Landmark.

# Biltmore House's Location

Biltmore House is located in the city of Asheville, North Carolina, in the western part of the state. The area is known for its lush forests and rolling mountains. In fact, Mount Pisgah, the highest mountain in the area, is only about 19 miles (31 kilometers) away from Biltmore House. The estate is also close to where the French Broad and Swannanoa Rivers meet. The French Broad River itself runs through the estate's grounds.

**LENGTH** The house's front **façade** measures more than 375 feet (114 meters) long.

**WIDTH** Biltmore is 192 feet (58.5 m) at its widest point.

George Vanderbilt named his house Biltmore after the town of Bildt in the Netherlands. The Vanderbilt family lived in Bildt before immigrating to the United States.

Vanderbilt chose the location partially for its scenic landscape. However, in the 1880s, Asheville was well known as a healthy place to live and visit. Its altitude and mild climate were thought to be good for people who were sickly. There was also spring water that people found healing. Vanderbilt thought this would be an ideal place for a house. His mother was often ill with malaria. He believed that this would be a good place for her to live.

**FLOOR SPACE** The floor space of Biltmore House takes up 174,240 square feet (16,187 square meters).

**FOUNDATION** The building's **foundation** extends to a depth of 29 feet (8.8 m). It is 14 feet (4.3 m) thick at its base.

# Outside Biltmore House

*Biltmore House's design follows the French Renaissance style of architecture. This style is known for its elegance and sense of luxury. Sculpted façades and pointed towers are just two of its features.*

**FAÇADES** Biltmore House's front façade is covered with a 6-inch (15-centimeter) thick layer of limestone. A variety of patterns have been carved into the limestone as a decorative feature. These patterns include leaves, **gargoyles**, and rosettes. Acorns and other symbols from the Vanderbilt family crest are also used. The rear façade is less ornate, but has two towers to serve as decoration.

**PITCHED ROOF** Like other buildings in the French Renaissance style, Biltmore House has a steeply pitched, or sloped, roof. The roof is covered with slate tiles, which were put in place one by one and fixed to the steel beams of the roof with wire. Copper **flashing** made the roof waterproof. George Vanderbilt's initials were engraved along the ridge of the roof with **gold leaf**. The gold leaf has disappeared over time.

**GARDENS** Several gardens, including the Rose and Italian Gardens, are situated on the estate grounds. The gardens were carefully planned to make use of both local and exotic plants. A series of pathways allow people to wander through the greenery. A fish pond and a lagoon can also be found on the estate.

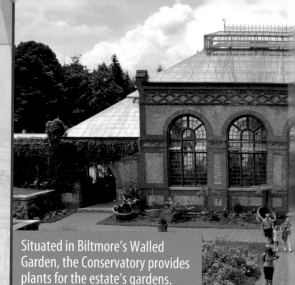

Situated in Biltmore's Walled Garden, the Conservatory provides plants for the estate's gardens.

Sculptures of fantastical creatures adorn the roof of Biltmore House.

Biltmore's front façade features a sculpture of Saint Louis looking over the estate.

The roof of Biltmore House contains no wood and is completely fireproof.

A **250-acre** (101 ha) section of the grounds has been set aside as a deer preserve.

There are at least **8 ways** to tour Biltmore House. One tour is narrated by Cedric, the Vanderbilt's Saint Bernard dog.

**11 million** bricks were used in the construction of the house.

Biltmore Estate has approximately **8,000 acres** (3,237 ha) of gardens and woodlands.

More than **6,000 weddings** take place at Biltmore House every year.

The estate grounds have about **22 miles** (35.4 km) of hiking trails.

**George Vanderbilt had a railroad built to bring construction materials to the work site.**

Biltmore has a combination of formal and informal gardens.

# Inside Biltmore House

*The inside of Biltmore House is decorated as richly as the outside. The rooms were designed to showcase the status of the Vanderbilt family and honor their way of life.*

**BANQUET HALL** The Banquet Hall is the largest room in the house. Sixty-four people could sit here for dinner. The room is 42 feet (12.8 m) wide and 72 feet (21.9 m) long, and the ceiling is 70 feet high (21.3 m). George Vanderbilt wanted this room to look like the main part of a church. Huge organ pipes were fixed to one of the walls to make the room look like an organ gallery. **Tapestries** from the 16th century adorn other walls. The three fireplaces have a carved **mantel** above them.

**GRAND STAIRCASE** The Grand Staircase rises beside the main entrance of the house. The spiral staircase has 102 steps, each of which is made from limestone. A **wrought iron** chandelier hangs down four stories in the stairwell. It is held in place by a single bolt that is attached to steel beams under the roof. The chandelier holds 72 light bulbs.

**LIBRARY** Vanderbilt was a book lover, and his library demonstrates his devotion to books. Two levels of books are contained within walnut paneling. A black marble fireplace runs from the floor to the ceiling. On the ceiling is a painting called *The Chariot of Aurora* by the artist Giovanni Antonio Pellegrini. It once hung in the Pisani Palace of Venice, Italy.

The furniture in the Banquet Hall was designed specifically for the room.

The Billiard Room is found in a part of the house called the Bachelor's Wing.

The bedroom of Edith Vanderbilt is oval in shape and features a gold and purple decor.

The library contains only about half of George Vanderbilt's book collection.

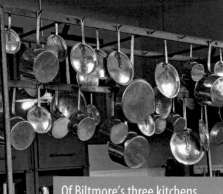
Of Biltmore's three kitchens, the main kitchen was where most of the food was prepared.

With more than 60 rooms open to the public, it can take **HOURS** to tour the house.

**Biltmore House used some of the FIRST LIGHT BULBS invented by Thomas Edison.**

Biltmore House has its own **bowling alley, gymnasium,** and **indoor swimming pool.**

The Grand Staircase chandelier weighs **1,700 pounds** (771 kilograms).

**The Banquet Hall covers an area of about 3,000 square feet (279 sq. m).**

The house has **16** chimneys and **65** fireplaces.

Found on the first floor, the Winter Garden is a circular room with an elaborately designed wood and glass ceiling.

The **Halloween Room** features murals of witches and goblins.

# Biltmore House's Builders

The construction of Biltmore House required workers with a variety of skill sets. Architects developed the concepts for the house and its gardens. Stonemasons worked at the site to cut and carve limestone. More than 200 workers were employed to create the gardens. Some of the workers were from Asheville. Others moved from northern cities.

## Richard Morris Hunt Architect

George Vanderbilt entrusted Richard Morris Hunt with the design of Biltmore House. Hunt was an American architect who had worked on other construction projects for the Vanderbilt family. Born in Vermont in 1827, Hunt moved to Europe with his family following the death of his father. He studied architecture at the École des Beaux-Arts in Paris before returning to the United States, where he eventually started his own company. Hunt quickly became one of the greatest architects of his time. He was well known for designing houses for wealthy people, and he also designed the **pedestal** for the Statue of Liberty in New York City. Hunt was one of the founding members of the American Institute of Architects. He died in 1895, shortly before Biltmore House was completed.

Today, Frederick Law Olmsted is often called the father of American landscape architecture.

## Frederick Law Olmsted
### Landscape Architect

Frederick Law Olmsted played a key role in designing the gardens and grounds of Biltmore Estate. Olmsted was born in Hartford, Connecticut, in 1822. His career as a landscape architect began when he was hired as the superintendent of New York City's Central Park. As superintendent, Olmsted was responsible for designing the layout of the park. This project soon led to other work, including the gardens for Biltmore Estate. As the estate's landscape architect, Olmsted planned the scenic driveway that leads to the house. He also designed the wilderness areas and the formal gardens. Biltmore was Olmsted's last major project. He retired in 1895 and died a few years later.

Richard Morris Hunt was the first American to be trained at the École des Beaux-Arts.

### Stonemasons

Stonemasons use a variety of tools to carve shapes into rocks. Two of their most common tools are the chisel and mallet.

Stonemasons are responsible for cutting and shaping rocks and stone. Some work in **quarries**, removing large chunks of rock from the ground. Other stonemasons carve patterns and designs onto pieces of rock. Once a piece of rock is cut into the proper size and shape, a stonemason is responsible for correctly placing it onto a structure so that it is safe and secure. This can be difficult. One reason is that the carved rocks can be very heavy. Another reason is that the work is often done very high up on the building or structure.

### Landscape Architects

Landscape architects design the areas around buildings. They use living materials, such as trees, shrubs, and flowers to create an attractive environment. Sometimes, structures such as fountains, stones, arches, and pathways are also used. Landscape architects arrange these elements in such a way that they have strong visual impact. To do this, they must know which structures and plants will look best together. Most landscape architects have taken courses in both architecture and **botany**.

Landscape architects create detailed design plans to show where certain plants and decorative pieces will be placed.

### Laborers

Most laborers know how to use power tools and other construction equipment.

From building a railroad to hammering materials together, laborers contributed greatly to the construction of Biltmore House. Laborers play a key role at any construction site. They get the materials into the hands of the people who need them. They do this by carrying the materials on their shoulders, carting them in wheelbarrows, and loading them onto trains and trucks. Laborers also help keep job sites clean.

# Building Biltmore House

When planning Biltmore House, George Vanderbilt had a definite vision. He wanted the house to look elegant and follow a European style. However, he also wanted to ensure the comfort of his family and guests. It was important to him that the house had the latest conveniences.

**PROPERTIES OF LIMESTONE** Approximately 5,000 tons (4,536 metric tons) of limestone were used to build the house. Limestone is a **sedimentary rock** that forms in shallow marine waters. It is a soft rock, which means that it can be easily cut and molded into different shapes. This makes it an excellent material for building. The limestone used in the construction of Biltmore came from Indiana. This kind of limestone has more than 97 percent **calcite**, which makes it stronger than other types of limestone. Indiana limestone is also known as a freestone. Freestones can typically be cut in any direction without shattering or splitting. This feature allows Indiana limestone to be used in many ways. It can be cut with a saw, carved by hand, or shaped on a **lathe**.

**ARCHED CEILINGS** One of the design features found throughout Biltmore House is the arch. Arches form entryways, frame windows, and shape the ceilings in some of the rooms. Architects use arches to support heavy weights. They support the weight of a building by converting the downward force of the weight into an outward force. This spreads the weight of the structure evenly across a larger area. To create the arched ceilings, Vanderbilt brought in Rafael Guastavino, an architect from Spain. Guastavino was known for his self-supporting arch and **vault** ceilings. This type of ceiling relied on tiles that were layered in a pattern called herringbone. The ceiling could support itself because the tiles formed a zigzag pattern. By following the curve of the arched ceiling, the tiles made the ceiling strong.

**MODERN CONVENIENCES** Biltmore House was equipped with many luxuries for the time. It had electricity, plumbing, central heating, a fire alarm system, and telephones. These conveniences were still uncommon in the late 1880s. Refrigerators were also rare at the time. While most households used ice boxes to keep food cold, Biltmore House had two walk-in refrigerators, as well as smaller fridges in the kitchen. The refrigerators kept food cool using a mixture of ammonia and **brine**. This is similar to the fridges in recreational vehicles today.

Indiana limestone remains a popular building material. Almost 2.7 million cubic feet (76,455 cubic meters) of this limestone are quarried every year.

A series of stone archways line the outside of the Winter Garden.

Rafael Guastavino's unique tiling can be seen in structures throughout the New England states, including parts of New York City's subway system.

Almost 10 million pounds (4,536 tonnes) of Indiana limestone were used in the construction of Biltmore House.

# Similar Houses around the World

Before construction began on Biltmore House, George Vanderbilt and Richard Morris Hunt traveled through England and France to find inspiration. As they viewed the many châteaus, or castles, and manor houses, they saw architectural concepts that they wanted to include in their plans for Biltmore House. The exterior of Biltmore House was inspired by the Château Royal de Blois in France. The inside of Biltmore was designed to look like an English manor.

## Château Royal de Blois

**BUILT:** 1845 AD
**LOCATION:** Blois, Loire Valley, France
**DESIGN:** François Mansart, Félix Duban
**DESCRIPTION:** A castle has stood on the site of the Château Royal de Blois since the 9th century. The current castle was restored in the 1800s following the **French Revolution**. The Château Royal de Blois is made up of several wings that were built over hundreds of years. A spiral staircase stands in the center of the main house. The staircase is three stories tall and is decorated with sculptures and royal emblems. The exterior of the Château Royal de Blois has the steeply pitched roofs and **turrets** of the French Renaissance style.

Over the course of its history, the Château Royal de Blois has been home to seven kings and ten queens of France.

# Waddesdon Manor

**BUILT:** 1877–1891 AD
**LOCATION:** Aylesbury, England
**DESIGN:** Gabriel-Hippolyte Destailleur
**DESCRIPTION:** Baron Ferdinand de Rothschild built Waddesdon Manor to be his country home and as a place to showcase his large art collection. The house was built in the same style as the châteaus in the Loire Valley. It has spiralling staircases inside, and its exterior features a steeply sloped roof and turrets. Lush gardens extend from the back of the building, while an **aviary** houses a number of exotic birds. Like Biltmore House, the manor had running water, central heating, and electricity included as part of its construction.

Waddesdon Manor became a National Trust property in 1957. The National Trust works to preserve historic places throughout the United Kingdom.

The Château de Chantilly was used as a prison during the French Revolution.

# Château de Chantilly

**BUILT:** 1880s AD
**LOCATION:** Chantilly, France
**DESIGN:** Pierre Jérome Honoré Daumet
**DESCRIPTION:** There has been a castle at Chantilly since Roman times. It was modified many times over the centuries before facing damage during the French Revolution. The castle was rebuilt under the Duke of Chantilly in the 1880s. The new château was designed in the French Renaissance style. It has several turrets and a roof with a steep slope. The gardens around it feature fountains, canals, and waterfalls. Inside is one of France's most extensive art collections, with 1,000 paintings and 2,500 drawings on display. The château's library contains more than 30,000 books.

# Issues Facing Biltmore House

Over time, all buildings need repair work, and Biltmore House is no different. However, Biltmore House faces issues that modern houses do not. Restoring the exterior requires specialized skills that most construction workers do not have. The interior contains antiques in need of special care. Maintaining the house requires both money and constant attention.

## WHAT IS THE ISSUE?

Many of the tapestries in the house had been hanging on the walls for years, where they were exposed to dust, sunlight, and heat.

Some of the artwork and furniture at Biltmore House are very old. They require specialized care to keep them in good condition.

## EFFECTS

The tapestries were dirty, fraying, and in need of repair.

Furniture and works of art would be less valuable without proper care.

## ACTION TAKEN

**Conservators** were brought over from England to repair, clean, and line the tapestries. A special workshop and water purification system were set up to ensure the quality of the work.

Housekeeping staff undergo a year-long training program before they are allowed to handle **artifacts**. They are shown how to move furniture, as well as the correct cleansers and equipment to use.

# Make a Family Crest

George Vanderbilt used symbols from his family crest to decorate Biltmore House. These symbols were carved into the limestone around the house. This gave the house a personal touch and showed that it belonged to the Vanderbilt family. You can create a family crest of your own by following these instructions.

## Materials
- Pen or pencil
- Paper
- Aluminum foil
- Modeling clay
- Plastic sculpting tools

## Instructions
1. Think of some items that represent your family. These could relate to interests that your family has, such as sports, hobbies, or favorite foods.

2. Take a sheet of paper, and draw a crest using some of the items you thought of in Step 1. Choose only those items that represent your family as a whole. Remember to put your family's name on the crest.

3. Take a piece of modeling clay about the size of your hand. Warm the clay by squeezing it in your hands for a few minutes.

4. Place a sheet of aluminum foil on a desk, table, or counter. Put the modeling clay on the piece of foil. Flatten the modeling clay into a square or rectangle on the foil.

5. Use the sculpting tools to carve your family crest design into the clay. If you want, you can add smaller pieces of modeling clay to your crest to represent some of the items. Mold these pieces into the needed shape, and press them onto your crest.

6. When completed, display your sculpture in a small frame for your family to enjoy.

# Biltmore House Quiz

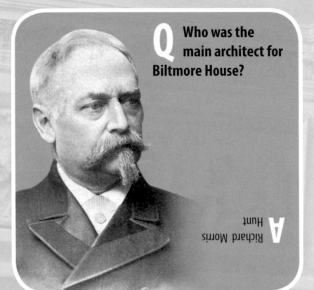

**Q** Who was the main architect for Biltmore House?

**A** Richard Morris Hunt

**Q** What style of architecture influenced the design of the house?

**A** French Renaissance

**Q** What type of stone was used to build Biltmore House?

**A** Indiana limestone

**Q** How many people visit Biltmore House annually?

**A** More than one million

# Key Words

**architecture:** the design of buildings and other structures

**artifacts:** objects that were made by people in the past

**aviary:** a large building in which birds are kept

**botany:** the study of plants

**brine:** a solution made up of water and salt

**calcite:** a white or colorless rock-forming mineral

**conservators:** people who protect objects from deterioration

**façade:** the principal front of a building

**flashing:** a strip of metal used to keep water from coming into a building or structure

**foundation:** the base upon which a structure is placed

**French Revolution:** an uprising that took place in France from 1789 to 1799, which eventually brought down the monarchy

**gargoyles:** stone carvings of monsters used as water spouts and to frighten away evil spirits

**gold leaf:** gold sheets that have been applied to a surface

**Great Depression:** a time of economic hardship that began in 1929 and lasted for most of the 1930s

**lathe:** a machine used to shape wood

**mantel:** the facing found at the top of a fireplace

**pedestal:** the base on which a statue sits

**quarries:** deep pits from which stone and rock are removed

**sedimentary rock:** rock that is formed when mud, sand, and pebbles become layered over time

**tapestries:** fabrics consisting of colored threads that have been woven by hand to produce a design

**turrets:** towers placed on larger towers or on the corners of walls or buildings

**vault:** an arch that forms a ceiling or roof

**wrought iron:** a form of iron that is strong but easy to shape

# Index

# Log on to www.av2books.com

AV² by Weigl brings you media enhanced books that support active learning. Go to www.av2books.com, and enter the special code found on page 2 of this book. You will gain access to enriched and enhanced content that supplements and complements this book. Content includes video, audio, weblinks, quizzes, a slide show, and activities.

## AV² Online Navigation

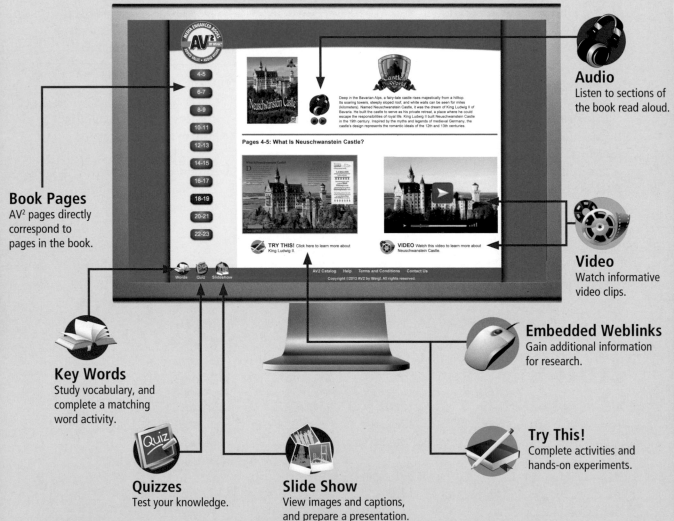

**Audio**
Listen to sections of the book read aloud.

**Book Pages**
AV² pages directly correspond to pages in the book.

**Video**
Watch informative video clips.

**Key Words**
Study vocabulary, and complete a matching word activity.

**Embedded Weblinks**
Gain additional information for research.

**Try This!**
Complete activities and hands-on experiments.

**Quizzes**
Test your knowledge.

**Slide Show**
View images and captions, and prepare a presentation.

**AV² was built to bridge the gap between print and digital. We encourage you to tell us what you like and what you want to see in the future.**

## Sign up to be an AV² Ambassador at www.av2books.com/ambassador.

Due to the dynamic nature of the Internet, some of the URLs and activities provided as part of AV² by Weigl may have changed or ceased to exist. AV² by Weigl accepts no responsibility for any such changes. All media enhanced books are regularly monitored to update addresses and sites in a timely manner. Contact AV² by Weigl at 1-866-649-3445 or av2books@weigl.com with any questions, comments, or feedback.